# Abounding Faith

30 Bible Heroes Who Will
Inspire You to Believe God
for the Impossible!

**Nancy Gavilanes**

D1397535

ABOUNDING FAITH: 30 BIBLE HEROES WHO WILL INSPIRE YOU TO BELIEVE GOD FOR THE IMPOSSIBLE!

Copyright © 2016 by Nancy Gavilanes

ISBN-10: 1523695854
ISBN-13: 978-1523695850

All rights reserved. This book or any portion thereof may not be reproduced or used in any manner whatsoever without the express written permission of the author, except for the use of brief quotations in a book review.

Scriptures taken from the Holy Bible, New International Version®, NIV®. Copyright © 1973, 1978, 1984, 2011 by Biblica, Inc.™ Used by permission of Zondervan. All rights reserved worldwide. www.zondervan.com The "NIV" and "New International Version" are trademarks registered in the United States Patent and Trademark Office by Biblica, Inc.™

For more information, visit www.AboundingFaith.com.

This book is dedicated to you, Overcomer!
This book is also dedicated to anyone who has ever
had the courage to believe God for the impossible!

# Contents

Introduction ........................................................................ 1

Woman with the Issue of Blood – Desperate Faith ........ 5

Abraham – Remarkable Faith ......................................... 8

Joshua – Victorious Faith............................................... 11

Noah – Obedient Faith .................................................. 14

Paul – Resilient Faith .................................................... 17

Job – Tested Faith ........................................................ 20

Joseph – Longsuffering Faith........................................ 22

The Centurion – Radical Faith ...................................... 25

Sarah – Mustard Seed Faith ......................................... 27

Mary – Humble Faith ..................................................... 29

Blind Bartimaeus – Outspoken Faith ............................ 32

Jairus – Interrupted Faith .............................................. 34

The Men Carrying the Paralytic – Compassionate Faith
................................................................................... 36

Martha – Resurrected Faith........................................... 38

Elijah – Unstoppable Faith............................................. 41

Peter – Crazy Faith........................................................ 43

Hannah – Extreme Faith ............................................... 45

David – Unshakable Faith.............................................. 47

The Samaritan Woman – Redeemed Faith ................... 50

Shadrach, Meshach and Abednego – Unwavering Faith ................................................................53

Daniel – Steadfast Faith ................................56

Mary Magdalene - Extravagant Faith ..............59

Simeon – Patient Faith ..................................61

Silas – Freeing Faith .....................................63

Joseph – Surrendered Faith ............................66

Esther – Courageous Faith .............................69

Ruth – Sustaining Faith ..................................72

Jeremiah – Extraordinary Faith .......................75

Samuel – Childlike Faith ................................77

Widow with the Offering – Sacrificial Faith ..............80

10 Powerful Bible Verses to Help Stir up Your Faith! ..82

Acknowledgements ........................................85

About the Author ...........................................87

# Introduction

*"And without faith it is impossible to please God, because anyone who comes to him must believe that he exists and that he rewards those who earnestly seek him" (Hebrew 11:6).*

They say children spell the word love, "T.I.M.E." I agree. And I would venture to say one of the main ways God spells love is, "T.R.U.S.T." Our Heavenly Father delights in us as we put our faith and hope in Him, especially when we are going through hard times.

The Bible describes faith as follows, "Now faith is confidence in what we hope for and assurance about what we do not see" (Hebrews 11:1). As Christians, we are called to walk by faith and not by sight, meaning, many times, we need to believe before we see the results. That is easier said than done!

But when we read about God's character in the Bible and read His promises, we can stand firm on His Word. When God gives us dreams and promises about our lives that line up with what we have read in the Bible, we are to grab hold of them even if at first they seem far-fetched or impossible. That just means we are about to get stretched!

God wants our faith in Him to grow!

Our faith deepens as we spend time with Jesus in prayer and reading the Word. And as we go through trials, we see God's almighty hand working in our lives. We get to experience God's faithfulness.

1

During some of the most trying and painful times in my life, when it felt like someone had pulled not just the rug but the entire ground out from under me, the only thing I had to hold onto was my faith in God. Every day was like a never-ending roller coaster. Amid the doubt, fear, and chaos, I clung to the truths that God is good, God is faithful, God is in control, and nothing is impossible for Him!

Those can all sound like trite expressions, but when you are going through what seems like hell on earth, those words come alive!

It was during that season that I would soak in God's presence and His Word and inhale His promises to me in the Bible. I learned that part of our maturing process is having our faith tested. That's how our spiritual muscles get exercise. It is how our character is refined so we can be conformed into the image of Christ. It is also how spiritual warriors are trained. We need to learn to use our shield of faith to extinguish the fiery darts that the enemy throws at us.

I mentioned some of the lessons I learned during that time in my life in my first book, *Waiting on God Well: How to Prevent Breaking Down on Your Way to Your Breakthrough!*

During that particular season of poring over the Scriptures, I found great comfort from the Bible personalities I will be sharing about in this devotional. Their faith in God inspired me and gave me hope when I needed it the most. I would read and re-read how God came through for them, and I would have peace that God would see me through as well.

When I would ask God why I was going through all these tests, one of the verses that kept coming to my mind was when Jesus was talking to Simon Peter before He went to the Cross. Jesus said, "Simon, Simon, Satan has asked to sift all of you as wheat. But I have prayed for you, Simon, that your faith may not fail. And when you have turned back, strengthen your brothers" (Luke 22:31).

Did you catch that? Jesus interceded for Peter to stay strong in his faith and exhort the other disciples once he was restored.

And so my friend, that is why I am writing this devotional. The Lord has graciously brought me through that chapter in my life. Now I am praying that your faith will be strengthened.

My hope is that this devotional will encourage you to believe God for the impossible! Dare to remove the limits off of God and watch what He will do. God is able! He is all-powerful and all-knowing. He is never asleep on the job. God loves you more than you will ever know and He is closer than you think!

The men and women you will read about were regular people like you and me. They had their flaws and imperfections, which you can read about in the Bible. But I will be spotlighting some of their defining moments. I want to give you just a snapshot of those times when they took a leap of faith and took God at His Word.

There was nothing special about them. The One who is special is God! He performed all the miracles in these stories. He can do the miraculous for you according to His will.

I pray that any storms you face in your life will help drive you closer to God. I pray your personal relationship with Jesus will continue to grow. As you abide in Christ, your prayers will better align with His desires for you.

Pray bold prayers and wait for God to answer in His timing and in His way. He will see you through. Jesus is the same yesterday, today, and forever (Hebrews 13:8).

Believe!

# Woman with the Issue of Blood – Desperate Faith

*"When she heard about Jesus, she came up behind him in the crowd and touched his cloak, because she thought, 'If I just touch his clothes, I will be healed'" (Mark 5:27-28).*

There are countless reasons why this nameless woman was an unlikely candidate for a miracle. She had suffered with an issue of blood for 12 years. Surely, if a cure existed, she would have found it by now, no? She had turned to many doctors for help, but instead of getting better, she got worse and was left bankrupt.

This woman, an outcast because her condition deemed her as "unclean" under the law, had no right to be out in public that day. How dare she even think of approaching Jesus and troubling Him with her hopeless situation?

Yet, she had the audacity to believe that if she just reached out to Jesus and touched the hem of His garment, she could be made whole! But that would require pressing past all the people and risk being embarrassed or restrained.

This anonymous woman could not be stopped that day because her desperate faith compelled her to reach Jesus.

Jesus felt power leaving Him. Imagine the woman's shock when Jesus asked who touched Him? She threw herself at Jesus' feet and confessed what she had done and said that she had been healed. Jesus didn't reprimand her.

Instead, He said to her, "Daughter, your faith has healed you. Go in peace and be freed from your suffering" (v. 34).

**Reflection:**

Do you know Jesus as your Healer? One touch from Jesus can bring spiritual, physical, and emotional healing. Is there something holding you back from seeking Jesus with your whole heart? Don't let doubt, depression, or discouragement stop you from reaching out to Jesus. When you invite Jesus to live inside of you, He is with you. He sees you and can heal the pain you are going through. He longs for you to draw closer to Him. Will you let your desperation drive you into His loving arms?

Woman with the Issue of Blood – Desperate Faith

**Prayer Starter:**

Lord, I admit I need help and healing in this area:

_____

_____

_____

_____

# Abraham – Remarkable Faith

*"By faith Abraham, when called to go to a place he would later receive as his inheritance, obeyed and went, even though he did not know where he was going" (Hebrews 11:8).*

Abraham, first known as Abram, must have had his retirement all planned out. He was 75, his father had passed away, and he was living in Haran. His life must have seemed pretty predictable. He and his wife, named Sarai at the time, didn't have any children. Perhaps he was content living in his comfort zone.

But God had other plans.

What must have gone through his mind when he heard God say, "Go from your country, your people and your father's household to the land I will show you. I will make you into a great nation, and I will bless you; I will make your name great, and you will be a blessing" (Genesis 12:1-2)?

"Go? Where, Lord?" he might have asked. But the Bible records no objections. Abraham uprooted his wife and nephew Lot without any set destination or roadmap. He believed God's promise, without having any evidence he and his barren, elderly wife, would ever have a child, let alone be the parents of a whole nation.

How did Abraham have the courage to take the first step? What led him to pack up his family and belongings and leave behind everything familiar to head to an unknown place?

Abraham had remarkable faith in God!

When he arrived at Shechem, the Lord promised to give the land to his offspring. That must have sounded ludicrous. The land was already occupied. He and his wife were aged. They were still childless. But Abraham believed!

After waiting 25 years, Abraham became the father of Isaac at the ripe old age of 100.

How did Abraham keep walking by faith? He put his trust in God!

"Against all hope, Abraham in hope believed and so became the father of many nations, just as it had been said to him, 'So shall your offspring be.' Without weakening in his faith, he faced the fact that his body was as good as dead—since he was about a hundred years old—and that Sarah's womb was also dead. Yet he did not waver through unbelief regarding the promise of God, but was strengthened in his faith and gave glory to God, being fully persuaded that God had power to do what he had promised" (Romans 4:18-21).

**Reflection:**

How do you react when God asks you to do something you don't quite understand? Do you refuse to act until you have more details? Do you barrage God with questions and ask for explanations or do you say, "Yes" to His will?

**Prayer Starter:**

Lord, help me trust You in this area:

_____

_____

_____

_____

# Joshua – Victorious Faith

*"The seventh time around, when the priests sounded the trumpet blast, Joshua commanded the army, 'Shout! For the LORD has given you the city!'" (Joshua 6:16)*

Joshua, who was Moses' aide, got to witness firsthand how the Lord delivered His people from Egypt. He saw the plagues. He crossed the Red Sea the Lord miraculously parted for the Israelites. He fought off the Amalekites. As one of the twelve spies, Joshua entered the Promised Land and surveyed the territory. However, only Joshua and Caleb came back with a good report. Though the other ten spies feared the people of Canaan, Joshua and Caleb had faith in God's promise to give the Israelites the land. They believed God had already given them the victory. Unfortunately, the people listened to the bad report from the other ten spies and gave into fear. They refused to believe God. As a result, the Israelites had to wander around the wilderness for forty years!

But God commended Joshua and Caleb for following Him wholeheartedly and said they would be the only two from their generation to live in the Promised Land.

After Moses' death, Joshua became the leader of the Israelites. God said it was time to lead the Israelites into the Promised Land. God commanded Joshua to be strong and courageous. He promised that He would be with Joshua as He was with Moses. God parted the Jordan

River, which was at flood stage during the harvest season, so the Israelites could cross over on dry ground.

Now they were staring down the walls of Jericho.

Joshua and his men prepared for battle. Then God revealed His plan. God's strategy was for His people to march around the city with the Ark of the Lord every day for six days. On the seventh day, they were to circle the city seven times and, at the sound of the long trumpet blast, give a loud shout. Such instructions must have sounded so bizarre to Joshua! How could he explain it to his army?

Believing God for the victory would take great faith. Joshua had to put aside his doubts, fears, and battle experience, and take God at His Word. If God said to yell at the walls, that's what Joshua would do. He was faithful and did his part, and God astounded him and everyone else as their war cry turned into shouts of triumph. The walls tumbled down. The Israelites rushed the city and started to take possession of the land God had promised Abraham and his descendants generations before.

God gave the Israelites the victory in subsequent battles because they continued to trust His instructions. As Joshua neared death, he encouraged the people saying, "You know with all your heart and soul that not one of all the good promises the LORD your God gave you has failed. Every promise has been fulfilled; not one has failed" (v. 23:14).

**Reflection:**

When you come across an obstacle to something you feel God has promised you, do you find yourself giving up or moving forward in confidence? How can you continue trusting God for the victory when you are facing your "walled city?"

**Prayer Starter:**

Lord, help me not to shrink back with fear in this area:

_____

_____

_____

_____

# Noah – Obedient Faith

*"By faith Noah, when warned about things not yet seen, in holy fear built an ark to save his family" (Hebrews 11:7).*

During Noah's lifetime, the earth had become corrupt in God's sight and was full of violence. God became grieved by all man's wickedness on earth, so He decided to wipe out mankind and all the animals.

But Noah found favor in the eyes of the Lord.

The Bible says, "Noah was a righteous man, blameless among the people of his time, and he walked faithfully with God" (Genesis 6:9). What a glowing description to have recorded in history about you!

God told Noah, already more than 500 years old, about His plans to bring floodwaters over all the earth. He promised to spare Noah and his family from the flood. He gave Noah exact details for how to build the ark that would keep him, his family, and all the pairs of animals safe.

So many questions and concerns must have run through Noah's mind! "Lord, do you know how old I am? How am I going to build this enormous ark? How am I going to gather all the animals? What will the future be like for my family? Will we really survive the destruction of the world?"

We'll never know, this side of Heaven, what ran through Noah's mind. But, his actions spoke volumes.

Twice, the Bible records that Noah did everything just as God commanded him (vv. 6:22, 7:5).

Noah had to push past any ridicule he must have gotten from those around him. He had to convince his family to get into the ark. He had to tune out any doubts that maybe he had imagined everything or misheard God. Noah had to set his eyes on God and the divine assignment given to him, despite how foolish or impossible it might have appeared. Noah had to choose to do exactly what God instructed him to do.

Noah was 600 years old when he and his family entered the ark to escape the floodwaters. They were the only humans who survived. God made a covenant with Noah that never again would a flood destroy the earth, and He set a rainbow in the sky as a sign of His promise. Noah went on to live 350 more years after the flood.

Over the years, songs and movies have been written about Noah. What set him apart? He had the faith to obey God even when what God asked of him didn't make sense.

**Reflection:**

Has God ever asked you to do something that made you look a bit foolish? How did you respond? How did things turn out? Is God asking you to do something that appears too grand for you to accomplish? Will you choose to obey God no matter what?

**Prayer Starter:**

Lord, help me have the faith to obey You even in this area:

_____

_____

_____

_____

# Paul – Resilient Faith

*"I have fought the good fight, I have finished the race, I have kept the faith" (2 Timothy 4:7).*

After his dramatic encounter with Jesus on the road to Damascus, Paul (first known as Saul of Tarsus) did a complete 180 degree turn in his faith. He went from persecuting Christians to becoming a believer in Jesus. Paul gained eternal salvation, but his fellow Jews rejected him, and soon both the Jews and Gentiles persecuted him. Throughout Paul's ministry he was beaten, flogged, imprisoned, stoned, and shipwrecked. You name it, the apostle Paul suffered through it.

So how did the apostle Paul persevere through all those trials, including pleading for the Lord to remove the "thorn in his side" and having his request denied? Let him tell you himself what the Lord revealed to him: "But he said to me, 'My grace is sufficient for you, for my power is made perfect in weakness.' Therefore I will boast all the more gladly about my weaknesses, so that Christ's power may rest on me. That is why, for Christ's sake, I delight in weaknesses, in insults, in hardships, in persecutions, in difficulties. For when I am weak, then I am strong" (2 Corinthians 12:9-10).

His resilient faith would not allow him to give up or denounce Jesus. He moved forward in the power of the Holy Spirit to accomplish his divine assignment. He would not abandon his faith. He preached salvation by grace through Jesus Christ and unknowingly went on to write more than half of the New Testament.

Paul learned the secret to being content. His focus was on Jesus and the rewards in Heaven.

"Therefore we do not lose heart. Though outwardly we are wasting away, yet inwardly we are being renewed day by day. For our light and momentary troubles are achieving for us an eternal glory that far outweighs them all. So we fix our eyes not on what is seen, but on what is unseen, since what is seen is temporary, but what is unseen is eternal" (2 Corinthians 4:16-17).

## Reflection:

What do you think would have happened if the apostle Paul would have given up somewhere along his journey? What do you think will happen if you give up on your journey? What steps can you take to keep living out God's plan for your life? Will you resolve to keep following Jesus regardless of what you might face?

**Prayer Starter:**

Lord, help me persevere in this area:

_____

_____

_____

_____

# Job – Tested Faith

*"But he knows the way that I take; when he has tested me, I will come forth as gold" (Job 23:10).*

Job's name has become synonymous with the word suffering. He lost his ten children all in one day, as well as his many servants and his cattle. He later broke out in boils. His friends, who were supposed to console him, accused him of bringing all this tragedy upon himself. They wanted to convince him he had done something to deserve his suffering. Even his wife ordered him to curse God and die!

There was no way for Job to know God had allowed all of this to happen. But God knew Job's faith would not crumble under the pressure. He knew He could trust Job to remain faithful to Him, come what may. Twice, the Bible records God describing Job to Satan as "blameless and upright, a man who fears God and shuns evil" (vv.1:8, 2:3).

Job had to choose whether to praise God or curse Him. There, in the midst of his grief and loss, Job proclaimed he would pass this test. He declared he knew his Redeemer lived (v.19:25) and though God slay him, he would hope in Him (v. 13:15).

Job's faith was tested to the extreme, but in the middle of his pain he still believed God would somehow, some way get him through. And God did. He blessed Job with more children and twice as much cattle and wealth as he had before. The Lord blessed the latter part of Job's life even more than the first (v. 42:12).

**Reflection:**

How do you react when a storm hits your life? Do you get angry at God and run away from Him? Or do you take your burdens to the Lord and pray and praise your way through? Can you trust God to work things out for your good as He promised in Romans 8:28?

**Prayer Starter:**

Lord, help me trust You even now as I go through this test:

---

---

---

---

# Joseph – Longsuffering Faith

*"And now, do not be distressed and do not be angry with yourselves for selling me here, because it was to save lives that God sent me ahead of you" (Genesis 45:5).*

At age seventeen, Joseph twice dreamed that he would rule over his family. His ten older brothers, already jealous of Joseph for being the favored son, hated him even more when they heard about his dreams. They plotted to kill him. But they reconsidered and sold him into slavery instead. Joseph ended up in Egypt. There he exceled in his master, Potiphar's, house only to be lied about after he rejected the advances of Potiphar's wife. He landed in prison where he met the king's cupbearer and baker. He successfully interpreted their dreams, but instead of helping Joseph out of prison, the cupbearer forgot to put in a good word for him. Joseph spent another two years in prison for a crime he didn't commit.

Joseph's dreams looked like just a fantasy. He was betrayed by his brothers and sold into slavery, wrongly imprisoned, and then forgotten. Joseph must have wondered if he had heard God correctly. He may have questioned what kind of future lay in store for him and if, perhaps, God had abandoned him.

The Bible records several times that the Lord was with Joseph and prospered him (vv. 39:2-3, 23).

## Joseph – Longsuffering Faith

We know Joseph still believed in God, despite his suffering. When Potiphar's wife tried to seduce him, he said he could not sin against her husband or God. When he was summoned to interpret Pharaoh's dreams, he stated that interpretation comes from the Lord.

It took longsuffering faith for Joseph to endure such hardship and to keep serving God even when things were getting worse and worse. But his reward did come.

Joseph successfully interpreted Pharaoh's dreams about the upcoming seven years of abundance and seven years of famine. He was immediately promoted to second in command of Egypt, the most powerful country at the time. Joseph was thirty when he served under Pharaoh and was placed in charge of the land. He stored up food during the seven years of abundance and sold the grain during the seven years of scarcity. It was during the famine that his older brothers went to Egypt seeking provision. They bowed down before the governor of Egypt not knowing he was their younger brother.

Joseph could have been bitter and unforgiving, but instead he recognized God had been with him all along. Twice he declared God sent him ahead of his brothers to help save their lives during the famine. It took years for Joseph's dreams to come true, but the time eventually came. Joseph's hardships were not in vain. He helped save many from famine and rescued God's people by providing them refuge in Egypt.

**Reflection:**

How does Joseph's story encourage you to maintain your faith in God, even when trials come your way? Will you trust God, even if things seem to be getting worse before getting better?

**Prayer Starter:**

Lord, regardless of how hard things get, help me keep believing You in this area:

_____

_____

_____

_____

# The Centurion – Radical Faith

*"The centurion replied, "Lord, I do not deserve to have you come under my roof. But just say the word, and my servant will be healed" (Matthew 8:8).*

As a Roman military officer, this unnamed Gentile man had no reason to think Jesus would do anything for him. But he still asked! He implored Jesus to help his servant who was paralyzed and lay in excruciating pain. The centurion must have been shocked to hear Jesus' offer to actually come to his home!

The centurion admitted he did not deserve to have Jesus set foot under his roof, but being a man of authority himself, he knew Jesus didn't have to physically be near his servant to heal him. Jesus just had to speak and it would be done.

The centurion's radical faith impressed Jesus. "When Jesus heard this, he was amazed and said to those following Him, 'Truly I tell you, I have not found anyone in Israel with such great faith'" (v. 8:10).

Jesus went on to say, "'Go! Let it be done just as you believed it would.' And the centurion's servant was healed at that moment" (v. 8:13).

**Reflection:**

God wants you to believe Him for great things just as the centurion did! Are you praying for something that seems impossible? God will honor that faith and will answer as He sees fit. Don't limit God!

**Prayer Starter:**

Lord, forgive me when I doubt You in this area:

_____

_____

_____

_____

# Sarah – Mustard Seed Faith

*"And by faith even Sarah, who was past childbearing age, was enabled to bear children because she considered him faithful who had made the promise" (Hebrews 11:11).*

Sarah, first known as Sarai, usually gets a bad rap for having laughed when she heard the Lord say she would bear her husband Abraham a son. However, Sarah was well past child-bearing years. She would have been around 89 years old.

It must have been a cross between the best news ever and the most absurd announcement she had ever heard. She, who was old enough to me a grandmother, would be giving birth to a baby, waking up for 3 a.m. feedings, and chasing a toddler around as he learned to walk?

People judge her for devising the plan to have her husband sleep with her maidservant to help God out. But she and Abraham had waited for years, and there was still no sign of the promised child.

However incredulous Sarah may have appeared on the outside, she believed God would somehow fulfill His promise to Abraham. In fact, she is mentioned in the Hall of Faith in the book of Hebrews. Sarah may not have understood how God would deliver on His promise, but she exercised the little mustard-seed faith she had. And that was enough.

Sarah looked away from her physical limitations and chose to believe God, and she was rewarded with her son Isaac. She is the matriarch of God's chosen people. Sarah hoped against all the odds, and received her promise!

## Reflection:

Has God promised you something that sounds so unbelievable you just want to laugh at it? Will you believe God is working behind the scenes to bring it to pass? Will you rejoice knowing God's Word does not return void (Isaiah 55:11)?

## Prayer Starter:

Lord, help me to see past any obstacles I may be facing in this area:

_____

_____

_____

_____

# Mary – Humble Faith

*"I am the Lord's servant," Mary answered. "May your word to me be fulfilled" (Luke 1:38).*

L ittle is known about Mary, the mother of Jesus. The Bible doesn't go into much detail about why Mary was chosen for the high honor of being the one to give birth to the Savior of the world. It only says she found favor with God.

When the angel Gabriel appeared to Mary, she was troubled by how he greeted her. The angel said, "Do not be afraid, Mary; you have found favor with God. You will conceive and give birth to a son, and you are to call him Jesus. He will be great and will be called the Son of the Most High. The Lord God will give him the throne of his father David, and he will reign over Jacob's descendants forever; his kingdom will never end" (vv. 1:30-33).

She was just a simple gal who was betrothed to an ordinary guy named Joseph. In those days, being betrothed meant she was Joseph's lawful wife even before their wedding ceremony, in every way, except physically.

Mary, likely a teenager at the time, was simply minding her own business. And then God interrupted her life. Although she questioned the angel about how she could give birth to a child if she was a virgin, she accepted the explanation. "The angel answered, 'The Holy Spirit will come on you, and the power of the Most High will overshadow you. So the holy one to be born will be called the Son of God'" (v. 1:35).

Mary could have dismissed the message, panicked, or even got puffed up with pride. She could have asked the angel to find someone else who was older, wiser, or wealthy.

Instead she humbly submitted to God's plan, even though that meant she would be disgraced in her community and she could have been charged with adultery and stoned for apparently cheating on her fiancé, Joseph. But Mary kept her eyes on God. She pondered things in her heart and even wrote a song of worship.

Despite all the unknowns, Mary laid down her own plans for her future and accepted God's will for her life.

**Reflection:**

Do you feel unqualified for what God is asking you to do? Does that job or ministry feel larger than life? Could it interfere with some of your own plans? Will you choose to humbly follow God's will or rebel?

**Prayer Starter:**

Lord, help me follow Your will in this area:

_____

_____

_____

_____

# Blind Bartimaeus – Outspoken Faith

*"Many rebuked him and told him to be quiet, but he shouted all the more, 'Son of David, have mercy on me!'" (Mark 10:48)*

As Bartimaeus sat by the side of the road in Jericho begging, he heard the commotion and discovered Jesus, His disciples, and a throng of people were passing by.

Bartimaeus didn't waste any time calling out to Jesus. His thinking may have been something like, "If I cry out to Jesus loud enough, perhaps He will hear me and help me."

Bartimaeus was not going to miss his chance to share his plea with Jesus. "When he heard that it was Jesus of Nazareth, he began to shout, 'Jesus, Son of David, have mercy on me!'" (v. 47)

The crowd reprimanded him and tried to make him keep quiet. Bartimaeus shouted all the more.

To Bartimaeus' amazement, Jesus did hear him and even called him over! Bartimaeus jumped to his feet, threw his cloak aside, and made his way toward Jesus. Jesus asked Bartimaeus what he wanted. He already knew Bartimaeus' answer, but he wanted him to say it out loud. This was Bartimaeus' moment. There was no way he would stay silent. In outspoken faith, Bartimaeus said, "Rabbi, I want to see!'" (v. 51)

Despite the opposition, Bartimaeus had the nerve to ask to be healed. Jesus granted his request and gave Bartimaeus his sight, saying it was his faith that healed him.

**Reflection:**

Do you need a miracle in your life? Have you asked Jesus? He already knows your needs, but He still wants you to ask Him just as Bartimaeus did. Jesus is the same yesterday, today, and forever (Hebrews 13:8). He still does miracles. Do you believe? Pray and let the Lord work things out according to His will.

**Prayer Starter:**

Lord, I'm asking in the name of Jesus that You would please:

_____

_____

_____

_____

# Jairus – Interrupted Faith

*"Hearing this, Jesus said to Jairus, 'Don't be afraid; just believe, and she will be healed'" (Luke 8:50).*

Jairus, a ruler of the synagogue, needed help. His only daughter, who was about 12 years old, was dying. His only hope was Jesus.

Jairus pushed his way through a multitude of people and fell at Jesus' feet. He begged Jesus to come to his house. Jesus agreed to go. But before Jesus could get to Jairus' home, a woman from the crowd touched the hem of His garment and was healed. As Jesus spoke with the woman, Jairus found out his daughter had died. There was no need to trouble Jesus anymore.

Jairus must have been angry, bewildered, and devastated. Why did this lady get healed while his daughter died? Life must have seemed so unfair at the moment. What could Jesus do for him now?

But Jesus assured Jairus his daughter would be healed.

Jairus must have felt distraught as he made his way home with Jesus. It looked like there was no hope. When they arrived at Jairus' home, mourners had already gathered to weep over the girl's death. Jesus told them to stop wailing because the girl was "only asleep." Knowing she had died, they laughed at Him.

Their unbelief was no match for Jesus.

Jesus took the girl by the hand and said, "My child get up! Her spirit returned, and at once she stood up. Then Jesus told them to give her something to eat" (vv. 54-55).

Jairus' faith may have been interrupted, but as He trusted Jesus, his faith was restored.

## Reflection:

What do you do when it looks like your situation is hopeless? Do you have the faith to still believe Jesus? That's what Jairus did. He had to look past his circumstances. When it's Jesus who asks you to keep believing, you'd be wise to obey. It's not over unless Jesus says it's over!

## Prayer Starter:

Lord, help me to know Your will and believe You without limits in this area:

_____

_____

_____

_____

# The Men Carrying the Paralytic – Compassionate Faith

*"When Jesus saw their faith, he said, 'Friend, your sins are forgiven'" (Luke 5:20).*

They remain nameless in the Bible, but these guys go down in history as some of the most persistent people. These men were on a mission to carry a paralyzed man to lay him before Jesus. The only problem was the place was packed. There was no way they were going to fit inside the house to see Jesus.

Now what?

The easiest thing would have been to leave in defeat. But they were determined to get the paralyzed man to Jesus. When they couldn't enter through the front door, they climbed up to the roof. Then they lowered the man—still lying on his mat—until he was right in front of Jesus!

What a spectacle they must have made! Jesus didn't mind. He took note of their faith. Jesus forgave the man's sins and healed him in front of everyone assembled there.

The group's persistence paid off. Their compassionate faith drove them to get the man to the feet of Jesus at all costs. And in return they witnessed two miracles! The man got saved and healed right before their eyes!

**Reflection:**

Sometimes stepping out in faith includes standing in the gap and praying on behalf of your loved ones. These men would stop at nothing to get the paralyzed man in front of Jesus. Is there a friend or loved one you are interceding for? Will you keep praying for them and wait for God to move in their lives?

**Prayer Starter:**

Lord, help me as I stand in the gap and pray for:

_____

_____

_____

_____

# Martha – Resurrected Faith

*"Then Jesus said, 'Did I not tell you that if you believe, you will see the glory of God?'" (John 11:40)*

Martha and her sister, Mary, and their brother, Lazarus, had the privilege of being Jesus' friends. The Bible says Jesus loved them. They must have seen many of His miracles firsthand.

So it's no surprise, when Lazarus got sick, the sisters sent word to Jesus that His friend was ill. Jesus got the message, but instead of rushing to Lazarus' side or even healing him from a distance, He stayed where He was for two more days. He announced to His disciples this sickness would not end in death, but would be for the glory of God! Jesus said He was glad He wasn't with Lazarus because now the disciples were going to have even more reason to believe in Him.

Imagine how heartbroken the sisters must have been when Jesus delayed His visit and their brother died! How painful it must have been for them to bury their brother. By the time Jesus arrived, Lazarus had been in the tomb for four days.

All hope was lost. Or was it?

Martha ran to meet Jesus, saying that, if He had been there, her brother would not have died. She believed that, even now, God would give Jesus anything He asked. She knew her brother would rise on Resurrection Day and that

Jesus was the Christ, the Son of God. What impressive words from someone who could have been bitter about her brother's death! In those moments, Jesus told Martha He was the Resurrection and the Life!

Martha must have believed Jesus, but that didn't change the fact that her brother was dead. When Jesus asked for the stone to be rolled away from Lazarus' grave, Martha balked, saying there would be a bad odor since her brother had been dead so long.

She had taken her eyes off of Jesus and was worried about her circumstances.

Martha and the rest of the mourners got a lesson in the miraculous power of Jesus! "Jesus called in a loud voice, 'Lazarus, come out!' The dead man came out, his hands and feet wrapped with strips of linen, and a cloth around his face. Jesus said to them, 'Take off the grave clothes and let him go'" (vv. 11:43-44).

Not even death posed a challenge for Jesus. Martha's faith was resurrected along with her brother. She learned indeed nothing is impossible for God!

**Reflection:**

With just three words, Jesus brought life back to a man who was dead! Think what He can resurrect in your life! God can breathe life, and health, and hope into any situation. Do you believe with God all things are possible as it says in Matthew 19:26?

**Prayer Starter:**

Lord, help me see Your resurrection power in this area:

_____

_____

_____

_____

# Elijah – Unstoppable Faith

*"Seven times Elijah said, 'Go back'" (1 Kings 18:43).*

The prophet Elijah was well acquainted with God's supernatural power. During the epic showdown against the 450 prophets of Baal on Mount Carmel, Elijah ordered that the sacrifice and altar be soaked with water three times. The water ran down the altar and filled the trench around it. Elijah prayed, and God sent fire from Heaven to burn up the sacrifice, the wood, the stones, the soil, and all the water in the trench (v. 38).

Now Elijah looked for the rain God said He would send to end the drought that had been going on for more than three years.

Without even spotting the first raindrop, Elijah told King Ahab an abundance of rain was on its way. He sent his servant to look toward the sea to check for signs of the expected showers. Six times the servant went but saw nothing.

At this point, others might have given up, but Elijah had unstoppable faith. He told his servant to go back again. "The seventh time the servant reported, 'A cloud as small as a man's hand is rising from the sea'" (v. 44).

That's all Elijah needed to hear. He sent word to the king to get his chariot ready and hurry home before the storm. Soon the sky grew dark, the winds rose, and the downpour began. The drought ended just as God had said it would.

Elijah prayed earnestly and then looked for signs of God's answer. He didn't need a monsoon to convince him God would make good on His Word. A tiny cloud was enough.

**Reflection:**

Are you frustrated because you don't see God moving in your life? Are you scared God won't do what He has promised? Will you continue to believe God even before you see the first raindrop? Will you begin preparing for your breakthrough even now?

**Prayer Starter:**

Lord, help me trust You to work in this area:

_____

_____

_____

_____

# Peter – Crazy Faith

*"'Lord, if it's you,' Peter replied, 'tell me to come to you on the water'" (Matthew 14:28).*

Peter often gets a bad reputation for being brave one moment and retreating in fear the next. The Bible doesn't gloss over his flaws, and rightfully so.

While he may not have always had all the right moves, one particular night Peter took the most exhilarating walk of his life. It was right before dawn, and the disciples were in a boat on the Sea of Galilee. The winds tossed them back and forth, and the waves crashed against the sides of the boat.

Out of nowhere, Jesus appeared walking on the water toward them.

The Bible says the disciples thought they were seeing a ghost and cried out with fright. Jesus told them not to be afraid. And then Peter spoke.

Peter said the unthinkable. He asked Jesus to call him out of the boat. Jesus agreed. Then Peter did the incredible. Peter got out of the boat, went toward Jesus, and walked on the water (v. 14:29)!

It took crazy faith for Peter to take that first step out of the boat, onto the stormy waters. But Peter must have known it was safer to be where Jesus was rather than in the boat without Him. As long as Peter kept his eyes on

Jesus, he was able to do something as astounding as walk on water.

## Reflection:

Is God asking you to do something that feels as scary as getting out of the boat and walking on water? Are you afraid you'll sink? Will you keep your eyes on Jesus and boldly take that next faith step toward Him and His plan for your life?

## Prayer Starter:

Lord, help me trust You enough to get out of my comfort zone in this area:

_____

_____

_____

_____

# Hannah – Extreme Faith

*"She said, 'May your servant find favor in your eyes.' Then she went her way and ate something, and her face was no longer downcast" (1 Samuel 1:18).*

Hannah had one desire that just couldn't be fulfilled. She longed for a child. Hannah yearned to know the joy of being a mother. Yet year after year her husband's other wife, who already had sons and daughters, taunted Hannah because she was infertile.

Hannah knew the One she could turn to with her pain and sorrow. During their annual visit to the city of Shiloh to make sacrifices and worship God, Hannah went to the tabernacle. She wept and prayed out of the bitterness of her soul. She vowed that, if God would give her a son, she would dedicate him to the Lord's service.

Her prayer was silent but so intense that, when Eli the priest saw her lips moving and no sound coming out, he accused her of being drunk. Once Eli understood her anguish, he said, "Go in peace, and may the God of Israel grant you what you have asked of him" (v. 17). Hannah left her petitions at the altar and went home a new woman. The Bible says her countenance changed. Her weeping and lamenting ended. She even got her appetite back.

Hannah chose to believe!

God remembered Hannah and in due time opened her womb. Her firstborn, Samuel, went on to become a revered prophet who served the Lord all his days.

## Reflection:

Are you thinking of giving up on your situation? God is an expert at working in seemingly hopeless situations. Are you delighting yourself in the Lord? He will give you the desires of your heart, according to His will, as He promised in Psalm 37:4.

## Prayer Starter:

Lord, show me what Your will is and give me extreme faith in this area:

_____

_____

_____

_____

# David – Unshakable Faith

*"David said to the Philistine, 'You come against me with sword and spear and javelin, but I come against you in the name of the LORD Almighty, the God of the armies of Israel, whom you have defied'" (1 Samuel 17:45).*

David may have been anointed the next king of Israel, but long before he got his crown he was still tending sheep for his father. No one took him seriously when he arrived on the battlefield to drop off food to his brothers and their commander. His oldest brother thought David was there just to get a closer look at the war between the Israelites and the Philistines.

Young David had come to run an errand but, when he heard Goliath threatening Israel's army, David volunteered to fight the giant. King Saul couldn't believe David wanted to take on the experienced fighter—without even wearing the king's armor. Everyone must have thought David was deluded.

But David had an unshakable faith in God!

David knew God had delivered him in the past as he fought off a lion and a bear that attacked his father's sheep. He was certain God would not abandon him as he faced this enemy. "The LORD who rescued me from the paw of the lion and the paw of the bear will rescue me from the hand of this Philistine," said David (v. 37).

David charged toward Goliath declaring that God was going to give him the victory. He defeated the giant with just his slingshot and a stone.

How did David have the guts to take on the Philistine who had terrified the Israelites for forty days? He remembered how God had come through for him in the past and trusted that God would deliver him again.

As Israel's king, David fought war after war and experienced victory upon victory. No matter how successful he was, David continued to rely on God and to trust Him for the win.

**Reflection:**

Are you facing giants of financial debt, health issues, work stress, or relationship woes? How has God helped you overcome past trials? Do you believe that God will help you this time as well?

**Prayer Starter:**

Lord, help me keep my eyes focused on You and not the giants in this area:

_____

_____

_____

_____

# The Samaritan Woman – Redeemed Faith

*"Then, leaving her water jar, the woman went back to the town and said to the people, 'Come, see a man who told me everything I ever did. Could this be the Messiah?'" (John 4:28-29)*

This unsuspecting Samaritan woman was simply going about her daily routine. She went to draw water from the well at noon, the hottest part of the day. She most likely had a reputation in town, which would explain why she was out while others were inside.

The Samaritan woman was hoping to go unnoticed. Then Jesus showed up. This Jewish man asked her for a drink of water. Jews didn't associate with Samaritans, and Jewish men did not speak to Samaritan women!

It was almost too much for her to comprehend.

When Jesus offered her living water, she was intrigued and asked for this water. Jesus asked her to call her husband, and she admitted she had none. Jesus pointed out she had been married five times, and the man she was with now was not her husband.

Jesus told the Samaritan woman that those who worship God must worship Him in the Spirit and in truth. The Samaritan woman knew that when the Messiah came, He would explain everything. Then Jesus revealed Himself as the Messiah.

# The Samaritan Woman – Redeemed Faith

The Samaritan woman had heard enough. She left her water jug and ran off to tell others in her town. She had enough faith to believe Jesus, the Messiah, had come to redeem her! She couldn't keep that Good News to herself. Many Samaritans from her town also believed because of her testimony. They went to see Jesus for themselves. "And because of his words many more became believers. They said to the woman, 'We no longer believe just because of what you said; now we have heard for ourselves, and we know that this man really is the Savior of the world'" (vv. 41-42).

This simple woman, who had a questionable past and was living in sin, had an encounter with Jesus that changed her life. As a result, she and many in her town were saved.

## Reflection:

What if the Samaritan woman had kept the Good News to herself? Instead she shared the news of Christ's offer of salvation with her community. Christ redeemed her when she put her faith in Him. Then many of her neighbors were saved as well. Have you put your trust in Jesus, the Redeemer? Have you shared Jesus with others?

**Prayer Starter:**

Lord, help me trust You as my Lord and Savior and share Your Good News with others, including:

_____

_____

_____

_____

# Shadrach, Meshach and Abednego – Unwavering Faith

*"Shadrach, Meshach and Abednego replied to him, 'King Nebuchadnezzar, we do not need to defend ourselves before you in this matter. If we are thrown into the blazing furnace, the God we serve is able to deliver us from it, and he will deliver us from Your Majesty's hand. But even if he does not, we want you to know, Your Majesty, that we will not serve your gods or worship the image of gold you have set up'" (Daniel 3:16-18).*

King Nebuchadnezzar of Babylon made a gold image ninety feet high and nine feet wide. He decreed that everyone must bow down and worship his statue at the sound of the horn, flute, harp, and other instruments. Whoever did not bow down in worship would be thrown into a blazing furnace.

But three brave Hebrew men, who were living in Babylon during the exile, refused to bow down and worship the statue. Shadrach, Meshach, and Abednego told the king they would rather die than violate God's commands. They knew God would deliver them. To refuse to comply with the king's order took unwavering faith. But they took it one step further and proclaimed that, even if God didn't save them, they still would not bow down.

The Lord did not disappoint them.

# Abounding Faith

Shadrach, Meshach, and Abednego were bound and thrown into the fiery furnace, which was heated seven times hotter than usual. The soldiers who threw them into the blaze were killed by the flames. Shadrach, Meshach and Abednego should have died instantly. But the king witnessed how they were miraculously rescued. He saw how the three men walked around unbound and unharmed inside the furnace. And they were not alone! A fourth man was with them—a man who looked like "a son of the gods" (v. 25).

Shadrach, Meshach, and Abednego came out without a single singed hair. They didn't even smell like smoke. The king realized that the God they served had saved them. He worshipped God and promoted Shadrach, Meshach, and Abednego.

The three men not only survived their ordeal, but thrived afterward. They didn't give in to the pressure to worship false idols, they faced the threat of death, and God rewarded them.

**Reflection:**

Are you tempted to compromise your faith on the job, at home, or in your community? Do you go with the flow or do you refuse to bow down? God did not fail Shadrach, Meshach, and Abednego when they stood up for what they believed. God will not fail you either!

**Prayer Starter:**

Lord, help me keep my faith in You and live for You despite the pressure in this area:

_____

_____

_____

_____

# Daniel – Steadfast Faith

*"Now when Daniel learned that the decree had been published, he went home to his upstairs room where the windows opened toward Jerusalem. Three times a day he got down on his knees and prayed, giving thanks to his God, just as he had done before" (Daniel 6:10).*

As a young man, Daniel was taken into captivity to Babylonia. Though he was being groomed to serve in King Nebuchadnezzar's court, he purposed in his heart not to defile himself by eating of the king's choice food and wine (v. 1:8).

God's favor was on Daniel. Over the years, he rose through the political ranks. Despite having great authority in a foreign country, Daniel did not back down from his strong convictions. He continued to worship the God of Israel.

When Daniel was perhaps in his 80s, he served under King Darius the Mede. Daniel was such an excellent administrator that King Darius planned to set him over the entire kingdom. The other leaders despised him. They wanted to destroy his political career, but they could not find any corruption in him. They knew the only way they could incriminate Daniel was through legislation that would force him to break the law in order to practice his religion. They convinced the king to pass an edict saying anyone who prayed to a god or man, other than the king, during the following thirty days would be thrown in the lions' den.

Daniel was faced with a life and death decision: follow the unjust rule or to stay true to God.

Daniel courageously continued to pray, and his enemies found him. They reported Daniel to the king. The king begrudgingly agreed to have Daniel thrown into the lions' den. A stone was placed over the mouth of the den and sealed with the signet rings of the king and other nobles.

God honored Daniel's steadfast faith by miraculously rescuing him from the lions. The king ran to the den first thing the next morning. He called out to Daniel, and Daniel answered. "The king was overjoyed and gave orders to lift Daniel out of the den. And when Daniel was lifted from the den, no wound was found on him, because he had trusted in his God" (v. 23).

God had shut the mouths of the lions.

The king issued a decree that all the people of the land must revere the God of Daniel. Because Daniel stood his ground, the Lord was glorified.

**Reflection:**

Do you feel like you are in a lions' den right now? Are you worried that God might have abandoned you? God has promised to never leave you or forsake you (Deuteronomy 31:8). Will you hold steady and trust God to rescue you?

**Prayer Starter:**

Lord, help me stand firm in my faith, especially in this area:

_____

_____

_____

_____

# Mary Magdalene - Extravagant Faith

*"Mary Magdalene went to the disciples with the news: 'I have seen the Lord!'" (John 20:18)*

Mary of Magdala wanted to be where Jesus was. She must have been overwhelmed with gratefulness to Jesus for delivering her from seven demons. During Jesus' time on earth, Mary Magdalene was one of the women who followed Jesus' ministry and supported Him financially.

Her love for Jesus didn't fade, even as He was being crucified. While most of His other disciples deserted Jesus and denied knowing Him, Mary and a few other women stayed nearby and saw where He was buried.

Early that glorious Sunday morning, Mary went to Jesus' tomb. Her devotion to Jesus would not allow her to stay away. That love and faith in Jesus, which continued even after His death, was greatly rewarded.

Mary Magdalene, who is named in all four Gospel accounts of the Resurrection, had the distinct honor of being the first person to see the risen Jesus! When Jesus called her by name, Mary recognized her Lord. He had risen from the dead as He had promised.

Mary quickly went to tell the others. She was the first to proclaim the news: Jesus is Alive!

Mary's extravagant faith drove her to keep seeking Jesus. As the Bible says, those who seek Him will find Him (Matthew 7:7).

**Reflection:**

Is your disappointment, bitterness, or sadness hindering you from spending time with Jesus? Don't let discouragement keep you from seeking Jesus' presence and believing Him. The Lord is close to the brokenhearted and saves those who are crushed in spirit (Psalm 34:18).

**Prayer Starter:**

Lord, help me keep seeking after You despite what's going on in this area:

_____

_____

_____

_____

# Simeon – Patient Faith

*"Sovereign Lord, as you have promised, you may now dismiss your servant in peace. For my eyes have seen your salvation, which you have prepared in the sight of all nations: a light for revelation to the Gentiles, and the glory of your people Israel" (Luke 2:29-32).*

There isn't much written about Simeon, but the Bible does call him a righteous and devout man. The Holy Spirit revealed to him he would not die until he saw the Messiah. How many years must he have waited? How would he even know when it was time?

Moved by the Holy Spirit, Simeon went into the Temple courts at just the right day and hour to see the baby Jesus as His parents brought Him to Jerusalem to present Him to the Lord as was the custom. Simeon had the tremendous honor of holding his own Savior in his arms!

Simeon was so overjoyed he declared he could now happily die since he had seen the promised One.

Simeon had waited years for God's Word to be fulfilled. His patient faith paid off. He lived long enough to bless Jesus and His family. He even prophesied about Jesus' destiny to His mother, Mary.

## Reflection:

Have you lost hope in a long awaited promise? Ask the Lord to give you faith that waits. Will you purpose in your heart to wait as long as it takes! It will be worth it!

**Prayer Starter:**

Lord, help me keep waiting on Your promises, especially in this area:

_____

_____

_____

_____

# Silas – Freeing Faith

*"About midnight Paul and Silas were praying and singing hymns to God, and the other prisoners were listening to them" (Acts 16:25).*

Times were tense. Testimonies about Jesus' life, death, and Resurrection abounded, and the rulers wanted to silence anyone preaching in the name of Jesus. Paul and Silas had just delivered a slave girl in Philippi from a spirit of fortune telling. Her owners, angry their money-making scheme had been ruined, dragged both disciples into the marketplace and told the authorities to arrest them for causing an uproar by advocating customs unlawful to Roman citizens.

Silas and Paul were stripped, severely flogged, and thrown in jail. They were held in the inner cell, their feet locked in stocks.

Both men could have unraveled. They could have wallowed in self-pity, given into fear, or become depressed. But they were too busy having an impromptu revival service!

Around midnight Silas and Paul were praying and worshipping God while all the other prisoners listened. What freedom and peace they must have felt despite being in chains!

Even God was impressed.

Suddenly the earth began to violently quake. The foundation of the building shook. The prison doors flew open and the prisoners' chains loosened. All the captives were set free. The jailer feared the consequences of having to tell his superiors the prisoners had escaped, so he drew his sword and was about to kill himself.

Silas and Paul stunned the jailer by informing him all the prisoners were still there.

Recognizing the power of the God Silas and Paul served, the jailer fell at their feet and pleaded with them to tell him what he must do to be saved. Silas and Paul told him he must believe in Jesus so he and his household could be saved. The jailer took the men home, bandaged their wounds, and his family received Jesus as Savior and were all baptized that very moment.

That night Silas and Paul were freed from prison, and the jailer and his family were freed from their sins by putting their faith in Jesus.

**Reflection:**

How you behave during your trials becomes a testimony to others. Are you having a pity party or are you praising God in your midnight hour? There's no telling how God will respond to your praise party! Who is watching you as you go through your trial? As you set a good example for those around you, they will want to know more about the Jesus you serve.

**Prayer Starter:**

Lord, help me worship You even as I struggle in this area:

_____

_____

_____

_____

# Joseph - Surrendered Faith

*"When Joseph woke up, he did what the angel of the Lord had commanded him and took Mary home as his wife" (Matthew 1:24).*

Joseph must have had plenty of plans and dreams about what his life was going to be like once he married Mary. He and Mary were betrothed. That meant they were already considered married in every way, except physically. Joseph must have been crushed when he found out that Mary was with child.

Mary was pregnant with someone else's baby?

Under the law, that was grounds for having her stoned to death for adultery! Joseph didn't want to further disgrace Mary, so he made plans to divorce her quietly.

But God stepped in to stop him. In a dream, an angel told Joseph not to be afraid. The child Mary carried was conceived by the Holy Spirit. The angel's words must have sounded so outrageous to Joseph. How could he explain this to others? How could he ever be a proper father to Jesus, the long awaited Messiah?

Despite all the controversy that would surround them as a couple, Joseph chose to believe the angel and took Mary as his wife. He later followed the divine instructions to flee from Bethlehem to Egypt when Herod put a warrant out for Jesus' life. And when Joseph got the divine message it was safe to return home, he packed up his family and moved to Nazareth.

## Joseph – Surrendered Faith

The circumstances surrounding the miraculous birth of Jesus must not have made much sense to Joseph. Although Joseph may not have understood that God was orchestrating events prophesied long ago, he surrendered to God's will anyway. Joseph yielded to God's plan even when he didn't see the entire picture.

God already knew that he could trust Joseph to follow Him. Perhaps that is why God gave Joseph the honor of helping to raise Jesus.

**Reflection:**

Do you obey God's call on your life or refuse to move until you see the whole story? Instead of arguing with God or insisting on doing things your own way, will you have the faith to submit to God's leading?

**Prayer Starter:**

Lord, help me surrender to Your plans even in this area:

_____

_____

_____

_____

# Esther – Courageous Faith

*"Then Esther sent this reply to Mordecai: 'Go, gather together all the Jews who are in Susa, and fast for me. Do not eat or drink for three days, night or day. I and my attendants will fast as you do. When this is done, I will go to the king, even though it is against the law. And if I perish, I perish'" (Esther 4:15-16).*

As a little girl, perhaps Esther pretended to be a princess but she probably never imagined she would one day become a queen. She was raised by her cousin Mordecai after her parents died. Esther was among the Jews who remained in Persia after the exile. When King Xerxes was looking for a new wife, many young women were brought to his palace. After a long selection process, King Xerxes chose Esther to be his new queen.

As queen, Esther must have had a pretty pampered life. But everything changed once her husband passed a decree to exterminate all the Jews living in the provinces of his kingdom. No one in the palace knew about Esther's Jewish roots. Mordecai had advised her to keep that a secret, but once he heard about the deadly edict he urged Esther to beg the king to put a stop to it.

Esther could have stayed quiet. Why get involved?

To go before the king in his inner court without being summoned meant risking her life. Esther had the choice to remain silent, hope her secret was not discovered, and see her people destroyed, or she could speak up. It wasn't a decision she took lightly. First, she told Mordecai to have the Jews pray and fast. She did the same with her attendants. Ultimately, Esther decided to go before King Xerxes, even if it cost her life. As her cousin pointed out, maybe God had allowed her to come to the throne for such a time as this (v. 14).

Esther's courageous faith paid off. The man behind the deadly plot was eventually exposed. The edict was reversed, and God's people were saved.

Esther's brave act is still celebrated today. The holiday known as Purim commemorates that the Jews were given relief from their enemies. And Esther is one of only two women to have a book in the Bible named after her.

**Reflection:**

How do you think Esther found the fortitude to approach the king with her request? Do you pray and fast when facing major decisions? Would you have the courage to stand up to a boss, parent, or other authority figure if they asked you to do something that conflicts with your commitment to Christ?

**Prayer Starter:**

Lord, give me the courage to stand up for You even in this area:

_____

_____

_____

_____

# Ruth – Sustaining Faith

*"But Ruth replied, 'Don't urge me to leave you or to turn back from you. Where you go I will go, and where you stay I will stay. Your people will be my people and your God my God'" (Ruth 1:16).*

After Ruth's husband died, her mother-in-law, Naomi, also a widow, urged Ruth to go back to her family in Moab instead of making the trek all the way to Naomi's hometown of Bethlehem. Naomi tried to convince Ruth she had a better chance of having a stable future among her own kind. She could still re-marry and have children, though not from Naomi's bloodline.

Or so she thought.

Ruth refused to leave Naomi's side. In one of the most endearing scenes in the Bible, Ruth decided to go forward into the unknown instead of shrinking back and returning to her old life. She begged to go with Naomi and pledged to stay by her side and serve the God of Israel. Ruth had no idea what awaited her in Israel. She was a Moabitess. Her people were enemies of the Israelites. She had no family in the new land except her aging mother-in-law. What type of life could a young widow have among foreigners? Despite all the obstacles, Ruth took many steps of faith on her journey to Bethlehem.

Although Ruth could have changed her mind and returned to Moab at any moment, her faith sustained her all along the way to her new homeland.

And God honored her.

Upon arriving in Bethlehem, Ruth humbly picked up leftover grain in a field. Unbeknownst to her, the field belonged to Boaz, who was a wealthy man of good standing, single, and a relative close enough to Naomi to be able to legally buy her deceased husband's and sons' land. That also included the right to marry her deceased son's widow, Ruth. Boaz and Ruth soon married, and they had a son named Obed. Obed's son Jesse was the father of none other than King David, an ancestor of Jesus.

Ruth, whose future looked so bleak at one time, went on to become King David's great-grandmother. She is one of the four women listed in Jesus' genealogy (Matthew 1: 5) and one of only two women who have a book in the Bible named after them.

## Reflection:

Do you stay along familiar paths or do you dare to allow God to surprise you? Will you trust God to guide you into new places and to provide for you as He did for Ruth when she started over in Israel? Whatever you are going through is no surprise to God!

**Prayer Starter:**

Lord, give me the strength to keep walking by faith and not by sight, especially in this area:

_____

_____

_____

_____

# Jeremiah – Extraordinary Faith

*"I signed and sealed the deed, had it witnessed, and weighed out the silver on the scales" (Jeremiah 32:10).*

God directed the Old Testament prophet, Jeremiah, to buy a field from his cousin. Sounds pretty ordinary. Except Jeremiah was in prison at the time, and the property he would be purchasing was in a nation that was about to be destroyed.

For years the Lord had been warning the Israelites that judgment was coming, and they should repent from their wicked ways before destruction hit. No one wanted to listen to what God was saying through His prophets. Jeremiah's message was unpopular. He was despised and imprisoned. Yet he persisted in speaking the words God placed in his mouth. He said God's Word burned within him and he could not keep silent (v. 20:9).

As the Babylonians surrounded Israel, ready to invade, Jeremiah followed God's orders to buy the field. Why purchase land in a city soon to be lost to the enemy? Because God promised to one day redeem His people and bring them back to the land He gave them.

God reminded Jeremiah, "I am the Lord, the God of all mankind. Is anything too hard for me?" (v. 32:27)

By buying the field, Jeremiah exercised his extraordinary faith. Jeremiah demonstrated that he believed God would be faithful to His Word.

## Abounding Faith

To Jeremiah's great dismay, the Israelites refused to repent. The people were taken into captivity. From that place of pain, Jeremiah is said to have written Lamentations. Despite the destruction that ensued, God remained true to His Word. After 70 years of captivity, God restored His people to their land—just as He had promised Jeremiah.

**Reflection:**

God's Word isn't always popular, but it is true! Will you take God at His Word? Heaven and earth will pass away, but the Word of the Lord will endure forever (Matthew 24:35). Do you believe that nothing is too difficult for the Lord?

**Prayer Starter:**

Lord, help me believe Your Word despite how impossible things appear, especially in this area:

_____

_____

_____

_____

# Samuel – Childlike Faith

*"The LORD came and stood there, calling as at the other times, 'Samuel! Samuel!' Then Samuel said, 'Speak, for your servant is listening'" (1 Samuel 3:10).*

When little Samuel was old enough to be weaned from his mother Hannah, she entrusted her precious boy to the care of Eli, the priest. Hannah visited Samuel at the temple on a yearly basis and dropped off the new robe she had made for him.

The Bible says Samuel grew in stature and favor with the Lord and people. Samuel lived during a time when it was rare for people to hear from God or have visions.

One night, while Samuel was in the temple where the Ark of God was kept, the Lord called him by name. The boy thought it was Eli calling so he ran to him only to find out it wasn't the priest who had said his name. Samuel went back to where he had been lying down. Two more times the Lord called him and both times Samuel ran to Eli.

The third time Samuel came to Eli with the same story, Eli realized the Lord was trying to get the child's attention. He told him to go back to his spot and, if he heard his name again, he should tell the Lord he was listening.

God did call Samuel again. With childlike faith, Samuel invited the Lord to speak to him. Samuel didn't question, argue, or ignore God. He opened his heart to hear what God wanted to say to him. He listened attentively and then he delivered the tough message God gave him for Eli and his corrupt family.

As Samuel matured, he kept his heart soft toward the Lord and remained open to God's promptings. He is regarded as one of Israel's greatest prophets. Over the years, Samuel sought God for direction, and God used him in mighty ways, including anointing David as king.

**Reflection:**

Do you take the time to be still and listen to what God is trying to tell you? Have you asked God to speak to you through the Bible and during your prayer times? God is longing to speak to you. Will you open your heart to hear from Him? Will you believe what He says?

**Prayer Starter:**

Lord, help me slow down and hear what You want to say to me, especially about this area of my life:

_____

_____

_____

_____

# Widow with the Offering - Sacrificial Faith

*"He also saw a poor widow put in two very small copper coins"*
*(Luke 21:2).*

Who was this unidentified widow? Her name and age are a mystery. It is unknown how long she was alone, how her husband died, or what her life had been like. All that is noted is she was poor.

The widow could have saved her money, but instead she made an offering to the Lord. Her financial state didn't stop her from being generous.

She probably had no idea Jesus was watching people as they put gifts into the Temple treasury that day. She may have felt intimidated by the others. How could her tiny offering ever measure up to theirs?

But Jesus was not impressed by the contributions given by the rich. He was struck by the widow who gave away her two very small copper coins. He pointed her out to His disciples. "'Truly I tell you,' he said, 'this poor widow has put in more than all the others. All these people gave their gifts out of their wealth; but she out of her poverty put in all she had to live on'" (vv. 3-4).

It took sacrificial faith for the widow to give that day. Years later, people still talk about her brave action and use her as an example.

**Reflection:**

Do you struggle with thinking you don't have enough time, talent, money, or other resources to give God? Do you feel you are lacking in these areas and wonder if God could use you? Remember God sees your heart! He can take the little you offer Him and multiply it for His glory!

**Prayer Starter:**

Lord, I offer up this area of my life to You:

_____

_____

_____

_____

# 10 Powerful Bible Verses to Help Stir up Your Faith!

Pray over, meditate on, memorize, and believe these verses! Then find more power verses in the Bible.

1.  "Now faith is confidence in what we hope for and assurance about what we do not see" (Hebrews 11:1).

2.  "Consequently, faith comes from hearing the message, and the message is heard through the word about Christ" (Romans 10:17).

3.  "In addition to all this, take up the shield of faith, with which you can extinguish all the flaming arrows of the evil one" (Ephesians 6:16).

4.  "I am the LORD, the God of all mankind. Is anything too hard for me?" (Jeremiah 32:27)

5.  "'If you can'?" said Jesus. 'Everything is possible for one who believes'" (Mark 9:23).

6.  "Therefore, brothers and sisters, since we have confidence to enter the Most Holy Place by the blood of Jesus, by a new and living way opened

for us through the curtain, that is, his body, and since we have a great priest over the house of God, let us draw near to God with a sincere heart and with the full assurance that faith brings, having our hearts sprinkled to cleanse us from a guilty conscience and having our bodies washed with pure water. Let us hold unswervingly to the hope we profess, for he who promised is faithful" (Hebrews 10:19-23).

7. "And 'But my righteous one will live by faith. And I take no pleasure in the one who shrinks back.' But we do not belong to those who shrink back and are destroyed, but to those who have faith and are saved" (Hebrews 10:38-39).

8. "If you declare with your mouth, 'Jesus is Lord,' and believe in your heart that God raised him from the dead, you will be saved" (Romans 10:9).

9. "Then Jesus said, 'Did I not tell you that if you believe, you will see the glory of God?'" (John 11:40)

10. "I write these things to you who believe in the name of the Son of God so that you may know that you have eternal life. This is the confidence we have in approaching God: that if we ask anything according to his will, he hears us. And if we know

that he hears us—whatever we ask—we know that
we have what we asked of him" (1John 5:13-15).

# *Acknowledgements*

I would like to thank my Lord and Savior Jesus who has proved to be faithful time and time again!

Thank you to my loving and supportive parents and my family. Mom and Dad, thank you for believing in me and my writing! To my sister, Sue, thank you for your love and encouragement and thoughtful edits. Much love to you, Dan, Steph, and Mark.

To Priscilla O. and Vernon L., I'm so grateful for your kind words and edits that helped to encourage me to continue moving forward with Book 2!

Thank you to the following friends who helped me keep believing and hoping beyond hope: Celine L., Jamary F., Priscilla P., Carmen G., Esperanza V., Christine V., Julie S., Lisy H., Kathleen M., Ana B., Lisa O., Dianna C., Delora L., Ruth C., and Kena A.

Thank you to Rev. Dr. Robert Johansson for faithfully pouring into me all these years! And thank you Overcomer, Uncle Toño, and Pastor Chuck V. for reminding me God still does miracles today!

To Pastor Jim Cymbala, thank you for inspiring me through your sermons during this season of my life. I am also grateful to the Brooklyn Tabernacle's Prayer Band members who helped to pray me through one of the most challenging times of my life.

## Abounding Faith

Thanks for your friendship, Nilufer D., Frank and Parija K., Jennie H., Shirley O., Sharon P., Heidi J., Christina P., and Diane W.

# About the Author

Nancy Gavilanes is a writer, speaker, life coach, and evangelist. Her first book is called *Waiting on God Well: How to Prevent Breaking Down on Your Way to Your Breakthrough!* Nancy has written for various publications, including *The New York Times*. She has a master's degree in journalism from New York University and has studied at the New York School of the Bible. Nancy has a passion for helping men and women grow in their love for and faith in God. She has been on short-term missions trips to five countries (and counting), has led outreaches throughout New York City, has trained as a volunteer chaplain, and has facilitated several Bible studies and small groups. To learn more about Nancy and find links to her books, blog, YouTube channel, online store, Facebook, Twitter, and Instagram pages, visit her website www.AboundingFaith.com.

What are you waiting on God for? Are you frustrated or anxious because you don't see God moving in your life? Are you tempted to give up and walk away from all that God has promised you? Don't quit in the middle of your journey! Choose to run to God, lean on Him, trust Him, and purpose in your heart to wait on God no matter how long it takes. *Waiting on God Well: How to Prevent Breaking Down on Your Way to Your Breakthrough* provides insightful tips, practical action steps, and inspiring Bible verses to encourage you to keep walking through whatever valley, desert, or wilderness you are in. This book will help you not just go through your situation but grow through it.

32529784R00055

Made in the USA
San Bernardino, CA
08 April 2016